THE

Giant

Killers

What killed the GIANT in Your man?

Dr. Cedric M. White Sr.

The Giant Killers

Dr. Cedric White
7951 Collin McKinney Parkway #3065 McKinney, Texas 75070

www.cedricwhiteministries.net
This book is available at quantity discounts for bulk purchases.

Printed in the United States of America.

Unless otherwise indicated Scriptures are taken from New King James Version, Amplified Version, and New International Version of the Bible.

Requests for information should be addressed to the above address.

Book Production: Krystal Lee Enterprises (KLE)

Cover Design: Dr. Cedric White

I dedicate this book to my sons, Cedric Jr., La Brandon, Justin, and Aaron Holden Jr. I pray that you will become better men than me. I pray your giant never dies; but if it does you have this book to help you through. I pray that God protects and guides you all as you navigate through your lives. Remember, Daddy will always love you and want the best for you.

ACKNOWLEDGMENTS

First and for most I would like to thank the Father for covering and keeping me through the process of writing and publishing this book.

To The Holy Spirit, my Teacher, Friend, and Guide through some of the most difficult and challenging times in my life, I promise we will always be together. I cannot see life without You.

Jesus, I cannot begin to explain what You mean to me and the joy I have just to serve You. I can remember the day You told me the reason You called me to ministry. Thank You for being patient with me when everyone else gave up on me.

To my wife, Tangela, I want the world to know you saved my life when you obeyed God by sowing into me. You changed my life with the most pure love I have ever experienced. I will spend the rest of my life showing you how much I love and appreciate you. RB, I will always love you.

Finally, I acknowledge all the women I have hurt throughout my life. If you are reading this book, I ask you for forgiveness and I pray that this open request for forgiveness brings closure and healing to your life. I promise I am a better man to my wife and I treat her with the love and respect she deserves. Please hear my heart. I sincerely apologize and I pray that you would please find it in your heart to forgive me.

CONTENTS

INTRODUCTION

I wrote this book because I knew that I was not the only man living in a silent hell of pain from the past. My process was not a pretty one and I did not always do the right thing or even follow the plan The Father laid out for me. But I am glad The Lord showed grace and mercy towards me and saved my life even when I didn't want to be saved. This book is for men and the women that love them. For women, I'm not teaching you how to think like a man but how to understand and help your man.

CHAPTER ONE

THE GIANT WITHIN

*When Eliab, David's oldest brother,
heard him speaking with the men, he burned with
anger at him and asked, "Why have you come down
here? And*

*with whom did you leave those few sheep in the
wilderness? I know how conceited you are and how
wicked your heart is; you came down
only to watch the battle."*

1 Samuel 17:28

Inside every man is a giant. A force if you will, that makes him the man that he is. In many cases, the giant is not yet killed but is on its way to being killed. In other cases the giant is already dead, has resurrected, and becomes a hybrid of a giant; or a creation of what killed the original giant in the first place. We have to identify where you or your man is currently. I know this may sound strange and a huge problem is, we as men, do not know when our giant has been killed. We just react to the process of our giant dying and then we become something completely different after the process is done.

Before proceeding, I must convey that because a man is a being that lives in a body with a soul, the giant that has been killed cannot stay dead; it must rise again. In most cases, the giant rises to become a hater of what killed it in the first place. This makes the man almost impossible to understand, live with, or love. When the giant is killed, what dies is that man's essence of what makes him who he is. His drive to succeed, desire to love, to be connected with a helpmate, his willingness to be open, to trust and fight to live...dies. Let us look at these symptoms in more detail:

1. Drive to Succeed

When the giant has been killed, the man loses all drive to be better. He begins to accept where he is in life, no matter how unfulfilled he is or becomes. He creates a false reality in his mind that life is never going to get better no matter what he does or what anybody says.

This can be very frustrating to the women in his life because no matter how much they try to encourage him, he does not hear it. Actually, it is not that he does not hear; it is that he has created a lying reality that has trapped him to where he does not believe.

Pro. 23:7 For as he thinketh in his heart, so is he: Eat and drink, saith he to thee; but his heart is not with thee.

2. His Desire to Love

When the giant has been killed, the man loses his desire to love or be loved. After the giant has been killed in a man, it is almost impossible for that man to love again. Especially if it was a broken heart that killed his giant in the first place.

(Important note) It is not that the man doesn't want to love; it is just that he cannot. He is literally unable to love because of the reality he has been created in his heart and mind. What we must understand is that men carry every past hurt that happened to them; every person that hurt them is being carried inside of them. When a similar situation arises, every past hurt is literally relived all over again.

Can you imagine how that feels—to have every past hurt relived in one's mind, will, and emotions all

9

over again at one time? This is why men try to shield themselves from loving, because in their mind, it is only a matter of time before they are hurt again. I am not saying it is right; rather, I want to convey that understanding is necessary before this phenomenon repeats itself.

3. His Desire to Marry

When the giant is killed in a man, he loses his desire to get married because he has lost all belief in himself. He feels that he is damaged 'goods' and that no woman would ever want him. He creates this reality that no one will ever love him nor will he expect to find it. In some cases, the man does not want to get married; he just wants to hold on to someone so he does not have to be alone. He has no real intentions on marrying this woman. He may give her everything she needs, but will not ever make that step of commitment.

This is the case where we see so many women get hurt, because the woman puts her all into a relationship that really has no future. This causes her to get caught in a viscous cycle of lies and deceit.

Ladies, it's not you. It's that he has created a world that is set up to protect him from any further pain. It involves keeping you at arms length because letting you get close means that he has to become vulnerable to you. This puts him back in the situation that killed his giant in the first place. In his mind he must protect himself by any means necessary.

4. Cannot Trust

One of the most devastating and debilitating symptoms is the inability to trust. This makes him put himself in a box, shielding him from the outside world; thus making him an island. What he fails to see is the mechanism that has been set up to protect him, is the very thing that will keep him from being free. The pain he continues to hold and try to suppress. The truth of the matter is when he puts himself in a box, he is unable to release anything.

The result is all of the pain, hurt, and disappointment that killed his giant, now serves as a reminder because his emotional garbage is stuck inside the box with him. This is very toxic to the spiritual, mental, emotional, and even physical development of the man. With all that is locked away and unable to be touched by outside forces (positive or negative), it becomes increasingly hard for that man to intelligently process what is going on with him; thus making him a prisoner of his own negative mindset and thoughts.

One of the most devastating and debilitating symptoms is the inability to trust. This makes him put himself in a box, shielding him from the outside world; thus making him an island.

The real factor in men not being able to love is they have lost the capacity to trust, and we know that without trust it is impossible to love; not just someone else but to love oneself. The apparent inability to trust oneself is the major sign that a man cannot and will not trust anyone else. This makes it hard for him to love himself, let alone love another.

5. Fight or Want to Live

By far, this symptom is the most dangerous, because it impacts how he can care about another. The pain gets so deep and hurts so badly, that he gets to the point where his heart and his spirit become broken. I cannot express the danger of this symptom enough, mainly because I can remember living this in my own life. A broken spirit can mean a broken life, relationships, heart.

I Gave Up

My personal experiences best explains this section. I talk about my state of mind later in the book; however, for the sake of this topic, I will give an inside view of where I was mentally and spiritually. I must say that by most men's standards, I was the man! I could have been intimate with any woman that I wanted. It was only a façade, a front because I was really dead inside. Basically, I had given up on life, love, ministry and I had no desire to live or do anything. I was at a point in my spiritual walk with God that I felt so much like a failure that I felt that even God had given up on me. I was broke, homeless, and living in my car.

I recall meeting my children's mother to see my sons, and they asked, "Why cant we spend the night with you?" I had to be as honest with them as possible without letting them know I had no place to live. I can remember the days of parking in the lot of the Intown Suites and friends' homes. These locations made me feel safe enough to get a good night's sleep even though not knowing where my next meal was coming from troubled me. I hear people complain and moan about not having what they want, but after living without what I needed, I appreciate the little things.

During this time of my life, I must confess that I was grasping for any and everything that would give me just an inkling of hope. I feared making a decision that would destroy me. I know the question, "You have an education, talents, and yet you allowed yourself to get this low. Why?" All I can say is that it had nothing to do with my education, talent, or the call of God on my life. It had more to do with my inability to deal with the pain that I suppressed for too long in my life. I could not take it anymore. It came to a point where I could no longer act like I was okay. I was at a state of breakdown and destruction, and only God could help me. I wanted to die; I even tried to kill myself six times before the Lord worked a miracle in my life, which I speak about later in this book.

If a man is involved with destructive behavior and stops to better his life, once his giant is in the process of being killed, he defaults back to his past nature. It is not that he hasn't changed, but he goes back because that is the only thing with which he has to protect himself. This man has lost the essence of who and what he is, so it is natural that he does not care about what happens to him. He has been hurt so badly that he does not know how to comprehend or understand what is happening to him. All he knows is that it hurts and he must stop it.

At this moment, I must interject and state that the process of a man's giant dying is an emotionally devastating time for him. The essence of who he is is dying. The very thing that makes him a man is dying, and he has no idea how to deal with it or how to stop it. However, in Jesus' name, every woman will know how to minister this effectively to any man that is going through this painful process.

I want to state that I did not write this book because to sound good, for acclaims as a author, for money because it is juicy subject. Rather, I wrote this book because I live every word and it is my prayer that readers will gain a revelation. Understanding this process and how to administer help to a dying man is my goal.

Real Life Experience

Life can ditch out unthinkable circumstances. The things I experienced cannot be easily explained. I lived through it and in hindsight that the guidance of the Holy Ghost revealed, I am able to understand what happened to me. If I would have known the power of His guidance then, I would have been able to get out of it before it started.

There are three instances that I can remember that killed the giant in me. It is important to understand that the giant can be killed, raised, and killed again, as long as bad things keep happening to that man. In this book, I offer the necessary tools in order to accurately diagnose and minister to a dying giant before it gets out of hand.

Instance One:

The first time I can remember is when I was 11 years old. It was right before I was called to preach. I really think that God called me to preach because no one else wanted me. So the Father, in His infinite love, decided to call me to preach His Gospel. Well, I was molested between the ages of 11 and 13. It was a very hard time in my life and in some cases I still deal with that today. Thank God for healing. Nevertheless, it killed my giant early.

Because of this molestation, I became very untrusting and I began to engage in destructive behaviors. It is important to note that when a man's giant has been killed, the first thing that he does is engage in destructive behaviors. I will not spend too much time on this because I talk about it in more detail in the chapter, "He Touched me, Not God."

Instances Two and Three:

The reason I put these two together is because they are connected. It is important to state at this time that I have been married three times; two failed in impressive fashion and the third has been the best thing that ever happened to me. I will talk about what happened in my 2 failed marriages because it is the most significant to the subject matter of this book. I recall a conversation with my ex-wife in the Intown Suites. We were separated at the time and she told me that it was over. She did not want me or to be married to me anymore. Weeks prior to this conversation, she started spending time with another man and said many hurtful things to me. My giant was well on its way to dying before this major breakdown.

During this time my mindset was damaged. The woman that I pledged my life to just told me that it was over and that I should move on with someone else. The pain was incredible as my heart and my spirit was broken. It was more painful than when I was molested. I began to experience many emotions sadness, anger, and brokenness. At this point, my giant was totally dead.

It is important to remember that when the giant in a man is dying, it is the essence of that man that's dying. He must return to the core of himself because

*there is nothing else he can turn to. He returns to
what he really is or the biggest part of himself. Let
me explain, if he was once the thug type, when his
giant dies, he will default back to just that.
Likewise, if he is called to preach, he will default to
that. The thing to remember is that whatever is his
core self, that is what he will default to--good or
bad.*

In the midst of this very dark period, I met a young
lady that was totally supportive and counseled me
about staying with my wife. However, things turned
more personal and grew to something more. This
time period was after my ex-wife kept telling me
that it was over. In my mind, I created a world
without my ex-wife because I was forced to deal
with the reality that my marriage was over.

I must admit that it is never a good idea to pursue
another relationship while still in pain over the old
one; it only adds to the confusion and in most cases
cause more pain in the long run.

After my ex-wife told me that she did not want me
and with me beginning a new relationship, my ex-
wife returned to tell me that she did not truly mean
it. Despite spending so much time with her new
male friend, she wanted us back. I believed I had
already dealt with the ending of my marriage. Now
I was dating a new woman and thinking if I pulled
the plug too soon on the relationship with my ex-
wife.

I realized that the giant in me was trying to get up and things were starting to happen good for me. My online radio station was doing great and the church I was pastoring had just started to rejuvenate. I was still dealing with the pain of my ex- wife being with another man; but no matter what I was committed to the will of God.

As my giant began to rise, I was killed again. I found out that the woman I was dating was lying about her availability and intentions with me. I was heartbroken and did not share my findings with anyone. I just kept it all in—all of the pain and disappointment inside was slowly killing my giant yet again. I think I came to one of the deepest lows ever. I relived every hurting moment in my life regardless if I wanted to or not. I felt small and began to accept I did not matter to anyone.

I found myself at a gas station—crying while sitting at a payphone and begging God to please help me. At this moment I received the revelation about the giant killers. The giant in me had been killed so many times until I had a hybrid giant. Although because I allowed God to come in and save me from myself, I still had to do some work with God to be restored. This revelation was not realized over night, but took 3 years and I had to marry the right woman.

Men must understand that we can evolve. God can raise our giant and give us a new life. All that we have to do is allow him to save us from ourselves.

The journey through my story in this book will instill the knowledge to achieve emotional and spiritual healing. My brothers, there is life after our giant dies. God wants so badly to help but we must ask Him for the help to be delivered!

A Brief Look At Some Causes

There are many things that can injure a giant in a man. Let us focus on the most common things that can kill a giant in a man.

1. Abuse (Physical, Emotional, and Verbal):

Although this normally happens when the man is young, it is equally devastating as they age because this is something that the man will carry with him all of his life. Words will ultimately affect every area of his life if he does not deal with the problem or avoids truth. When this happens, the giant in the man has no time to grow before it is killed, so the man grows up with a hybrid giant. This is why we have men growing up with unnatural affections for another man. Not only is this the cause for many men becoming homosexual or having homosexual tendencies, it also gives that man an inferiority complex before he even has a chance to grow into who and what he was called to be.

2. Missing Father:

It is really important to understand the link between a father and his son. It is nearly impossible to grow up as a strong man when there is no role model to imitate. It is important that if the child's father is not in his life, the son will pick up the same tendencies and deficiencies as the men around him.

3. Pain from a Woman:

This is the most common type of giant killer. I can attest from personal experience. What ladies do not understand is when a man gives of himself; he exposes his essence to the recipient. He gives his giant—his hopes, dreams, fears, and all that makes him who and what he is subjected to her thoughts, opinions, and feelings. The problem is that women do not know when he has given her all of him because it is not openly identifiable. In most cases it is hidden altogether. What ends up happening is that the woman constantly asks him for something that he has already given; making him feel like what he has given is not enough. He pulls back and is lost, wounded. When he is gone, he is gone. He may come around, but his love is gone and unless God restores that love again, it is dead.

I understand that much was covered in this introductory chapter and it will take some time to properly digest all of this information. (If you have the workbook, please work through the section for chapter One at the conclusion of this chapter.) Be patient as you work through this book. It took me three years to get it and divine revelation from God for me to understand, apply the principles found in this book.

This book took seven years to start and complete because I had to face myself. This book is only possible because God stepped in and took me through the journey to healing and deliverance.

What I will promise is that I will be here during this journey and make the commitment to give all that God has given me on this subject. It is going to take the commitment of us all in order to achieve healing or understanding. Let us raise our giants together with the help of the Holy Spirit.

CHAPTER TWO

WHO KILLED MY GIANT?

Now what have I done?" said David. "Can't I even speak?" He then turned away to someone else and brought up the same matter, and the men answered him as before. What David said was overheard and reported to Saul, and Saul sent for him. David said to Saul, "Let no one lose heart on account of this Philistine; your servant will go and fight him."

1 Samuel 1:29-32

As I think back, numerous happenings killed the giant inside of me. I remember living with my mother at the age of 7 or 8. My stepfather's mother would repeatedly call me 'black catfish' because I was darker than anyone else in the family. At the time, it hurt my feelings but I ignored the insult and pretended it did not matter until I was older. It was this constant reticule by my family that caused me to develop a distorted view of myself. I can honestly say that it was the distorted and unfair view of myself that caused me to react to situations, circumstances, and relationships in a negative way.

The problem is most men will not openly reveal where they are hurting or what caused it. Men need to be encouraged, loved and feel safe to reveal the matters of their heart. Although men are strong the must at some point in life address the sickness that is killing them from the inside out.

I have been in ministry since the age of 11. I am now 40 and my repeated question to God was, "How can I preach life when I'm dead inside?" There are lots of men that are asking God on behalf of their families, "How can I lead when all I see around me is death—physically, emotionally, and spiritually?" The reality is that we have a nation of women who are frustrated and hurt because they are married or in love with a man that has a dead or hybrid giant within. They do not know the first thing to do to save the man they love.

Women all over the world are tired because the more they try to help their man, the more they both hurt. Women left me when my giant was dead and I could not blame them; but the right woman stayed and fought the battle with me. No woman can save a man neither should you expect them to rescue you.

The first step women must decide, is this husband, boyfriend, father, son or brother worth my time because you have to have hope for the man. To help, you must be educated, prepared to pray, and trust in the Lord. Restoration is only achieved with Jesus' help, because God makes all things possible if we only believe. This chapter offers a deeper understanding about what really happens when you have a support team equipped to help you battle your inner demons.

The Issue That Goes Unaddressed Will Kill Him

Many men are in a broken state of being. Most men sleepwalk through life never truly being healed of past hurts. Hurts may come from family, friends, a relationship, or even the church. The problem most men find is they have no idea of the source or how to ease the pain they feel. In most cases, these men live with others, attend a church, sleep next to a warm body, go to school, cook and may even preach in a pulpit. Men of today can live in a silent nightmare with silent screams that go unheard. If men took a poll, it would reveal nearly 100% of men have some type of emotional hurt that was never properly handled.

Unchecked and unresolved emotional issues can cause a man to do strange and out-of-character things. The saying "I don't know what has gotten into him!" is a common statement at this stage. The truth of the matter, these characteristics did not pop up overnight; rather, the traits were developed some time in the past but are now manifesting outwardly. It is possible this man did not have the courage or know how to resolve his issues.

Unresolved sexual issues for example can lead to a man becoming sexually deviant in that he has numerous partners. Unresolved anger issues are leading factors that cause men to become controlling and manipulative in their relationships. Unresolved father issues can cause men to devalue the father/son relationship with their own son. Unresolved self-esteem issues can cause that same man to not believe in himself and lose all drive to succeed.

These are only a few of the internal issues that can cause a man to exhibit signs of distorted behavior. Did you know that unresolved emotional issues are the most common cause for depression among men according to my 20 years in counseling. This deeply rooted pain men hide from others silently kills them. The overwhelming pain that I have endured in my life is tragic but God is a healer. I pray that He grants the healing I received through this revelation and also encourage you. Pain has a purpose in our lives. Everything that God allows in our lives has a purpose and is used to bring us into a deeper relationship with Him.

We cannot truly understand our destiny until we have gone through some level of pain. There are two schools of thought that I want to highlight:

1. Ontology – the study of being. Paul Tillich, a well-known German theologian, talks about ***The Courage to Be***. He writes, "One cannot find their being or come into their being until they have met opposition or have experienced pain." He goes on to imply that this opposition cannot be familiar but unknown. Courage is developed when we face unknown opposition.

2. Thymus – Plato's Republic introduces us to a word called *thymus,* which implies that within the inside of our being we have a spirited nature with a courageous element. This furthermore indicates we can yield intellect and power in intense times. In laymen's terms,

"When my back is against the wall, I don't fall away. There is a God nature in me that tells me that I can do all things through Christ that strengthens me." This tells me that when there seems no way out, because I use my intellect and heavenly power, I find a way to win. I have learned to win despite my challenges and looming failure.

The problem comes when the man is not taught his true nature. The nature process enables us to overcome and dismiss all negative situations that will attempt to stop him from being the best man he can be.

The Giant Killers Exposed: Abuse (Physically Emotionally)

This is a very hard thing for men to discuss. From the time we were born, we have been taught not to show any weakness in any area. I can remember falling and hurting my knee and my father saying, "Men don't cry; they suck it up." This is something that has been carried on into my adult life and for men alike. It is this inability to show real emotion that stops a man from truly connecting with his wife, children, and family. We have to be honest and willing to express our feelings because suppressing pain does not make it go away. Suppressing it not only puts us in a box but also limits our ability to face similar situations that arrive.

The reason most men do not want to talk about abuse is because it makes them vulnerable to their abuser. In their mind, by not talking about it, it gives them some perceived power to overcome it. This type of thinking is the devil's greatest weapon against men. The longer it takes for a man to deal with the emotions the longer the wait for healing. I have found (citation) a common denominator that abusers and murderers have unresolved emotional issues stemming from being a victim. Hurt people hurt people.

Let us explore what really happens inside that man. Men process things much differently than women. We internalize things that hurt us as long as we can before we lose it. The problem arises when we do not know when we have suppressed beyond our breaking point. The neglect of resolve and healing can breed violence, isolation, emotional shut down, and the lot.

Abuse is one of the hardest things to deal with because in most cases, the abuse happens when the man is very young. This pain grows up with the child and shapes his life. He becomes a grown man living like a damaged little boy. The scary reality is there is a child fighting back with the strength of a man. Male criminals guilty of committing violent crimes likely have unresolved childhood issues. When a man revisits an abusive memory in his adulthood, he may choose to fight instead of being a victim—he may even become the initiator.

Actions men take imply they struggle to articulate in words how current situations soar them to the past. This state of being I call *emotional atmospheric neuro-conditioning. In short,* a person is conditioned to behave in a manner to protect himself from further harm oblivious to any negative fallout from his decision.

What I am saying is that certain situations trigger the remembrance of what happened to him as a child, and because the issue is unresolved, he reacts as the hurt child instead of the grown man that he is now.

This mindset builds power that can influence positive or negative chain reactions. I will go further to say the mindset can be generational. Generational mindsets are merely mindsets that have been passed down from parent to child. The leading way to control the situation is the man must confront the mindset and decide how to channel his power. This power is best managed with a relationship with God in my view that makes change life lasting. It is possible to learn to direct your power because of the prayers and fasting of someone else so consider prayer even if you do not choose to do it.

Missing Father

Chapter 4 explores this area in great detail because I feel that it needs to have its own chapter. I am 37 (are you still 37?) and I have never had a father figure. I am sad to admit that at my age I still look for father influence. I sometimes sit and fantasize what my life would have been like if I had a father that supported me or give me advice. I compare my life to my friends who had fatherly influence and have noted the difference.

The Wal-Mart Epiphany

I remember one night in Wal-Mart shopping with my sons and their mother. My son Cedric Jr. asked me to pick him up and I told him, "Stop acting like a girl; you are a man—walk!" His mother got so angry with me and yelled, "You have to give them more than money Cedric—they need you!" I was a bit embarrassed but I thought to myself, "I have no idea what I am doing."   I never had a father so there was no one to teach me how to father. How can she expect me to be something that I never had?

I knew regardless of my past, I had to learn this dad thing the best way I could or I am at risk of loosing my boys. The truth scared me but instead of stirring flight it stirred fight. Like me, there are many men with children that have no idea of what to do. This is not an excuse to avoid responsibility. Instead, we need to show sympathy for those struggling to be fathers so he is not discouraged. This does not mean you are not honest with him. If my wife did not make me aware, I would not have known to change. I believe the church—men groups can help discourage men from giving up on fatherhood. Chapter 4 will elaborate on this topic and concept more.

Pain of a Woman

Chapter 5 – "She Hurt Me" discusses this subject in greater detail then I will here. There is nothing more hurtful or harder to get over than the pain from a woman. Once a man has been hurt, many do not know how to deal with that hurt. In most cases, he takes the pain and dishes it back out; case and point the womanizer. He does this because he does not want to ever feel that pain again, and he does everything in his power not to. Again, we will revisit this topic in Chapter 5.

I. Unrealized Spiritual Issues

I. Spiritual Deficiencies—It is important that we all understand that it is impossible for a man to maneuver through life successfully without the Spirit of God. The Spirit is the fuel we need to keep our spiritual life moving forward and not stall or shut down. We experience spiritual deficiencies when we lose our connection with God.

1. No prayer —the first thing that initiates spiritual deficiency is a insufficient prayer life.

2. Stopped Reading the Word—the second, not reading or studying the Word of God.

3. Absent at Church—the Bible says we should not forsake the gathering of the saints in the assemble. There is strength in numbers. I believe there is a shortage of men in church because submission is difficult for men. Many men today grow up with an absent father. The young men learn to answer to their mother in their youth and their own way as they grow; if the media does not shape them.

II. Unrealized Value

Unrealized value can choke out a man's giant to breaths of his life. There is nothing more destructive than a man that does not know his value. In most cases, it is not entirely the man's fault. As I can attest from my own life, from birth until death, society and the devil has engaged an all-out attack on the value of men. The reason men can so freely give themselves sexually is because society, someone, or something has said they are not valuable.

Even more dangerous, this erroneous teaching by our mentors have caused this type of thinking to spread out of the bedroom and into other areas of our lives. Conversely, most little girls are taught from a young age that their virginity is sacred and should not be given to a man lightly. However, men are not taught that they have something valuable, and that it should be given to anyone that will receive it. How can we expect men to believe they are valuable when they are taught to devalue their bodies?

III. Unrealized Potential

How can a man realize his true potential? Let's take a look at a two scripture verses that define man.

Isaiah 5:13 "Therefore, my people are gone into captivity for lack of knowledge; and their honorable

*men are famished, and their multitude are parched
with thirst."*

*Hos 4:6 – "My people are destroyed for lack of
knowledge: because thou hast rejected knowledge, I
will also reject thee, that thou shalt be no priest to
me: seeing thou hast forgotten the law of thy God, I
also will forget thy children."*

The problem most men struggle to understand is the
value God has placed on them and their lives. Most
men don't. Too many times men allow others
outside of God to dictate our value, which is not an
accurate representation of our worth. The deception
is of no affect by simply being said but when it is
believed.

*It is impossible for someone to respect your worth,
when you do not demonstrate your value. A man
who walks in the light can be seen no matter who
attempts to devalue him.*

III. Unrealized Enemy

A under estimated danger for men is to be oblivious
or under estimate our enemy. A startling
conversation I routinely hear and read, the White
Man is holding X Man down. Let us be clear,
racism still exists in America; however, it is not that
the White, Red, Yellow, Blue, or Black man holds
anyone down. It is only because of the limits a man
places on himself that he creates the glass ceiling.

33

Until a man stops blaming everyone else for his hardships, he will never go anywhere.

The Bible teaches us our enemy is not a man, but your beliefs—it's a spiritual battle that starts in your mind. That war is won or lost in your mind. Until we realize the source of our strength we will always deal with unresolved emotional issues.

Eph 6:12 – *"For we wrestle not against flesh and blood, but against principalities, against powers, against the rulers of the darkness of this world, against spiritual wickedness in high places."*

Too many times we allow others to place a value on us, which is not an accurate representation or appraisal of our worth.

In a fight, most men focus on the person, place, or thing that is causing the issue instead of focusing on the root of the problem. Our battle is spiritual so we fight spirits that attempt to control our thoughts and act out in our being. Men must be taught how important we are to the body of Christ and that the devil's job is to keep the giant dead. When your giant is dead, the devil can control your state of mind and defeat you.

IV. Poor Fighting Methods

Most men do not know how to war with the enemy. You have to understand and know how to silence your enemy.

Eph 6:13 *– "Wherefore take unto you the whole armor of God, that ye may be able to withstand in the evil day, and having done all, to stand."*

Eph 6:14 *– "Stand therefore, having your loins girt about with truth, and having on the breastplate of righteousness;"*

Eph6:15*–"And your feet shod with the preparation of the gospel of peace;"*

Eph 6:16 *– "Above all, taking the shield of faith, wherewith ye shall be able to quench all the fiery darts of the wicked."*

Eph 6:17 *– "And take the helmet of salvation, and the sword of the Spirit, which is the word of God:"*

Eph 6:18 *– "Praying always with all prayer and supplication in the Spirit, and watching thereunto with all perseverance and supplication for all saints."*

It is important to be able to identify what kills the giant in you or the man in your life. Proceed to section two in your workbook to determine and chart your findings. Once you identify what's killing you, you can properly pray, request prayer, and work through the solution.

CHAPTER THREE

THE WOUNDED HEART OF A MAN

Saul replied, "You are not able to go out against this Philistine and fight him; you are only a young man, and he has been a warrior from his youth." But David said to

Saul, "Your servant has been keeping his father's sheep. When a lion or a bear came and carried off a sheep from the flock, I went after it, struck it and rescued the sheep from its mouth. When it turned on me, I seized it by its hair, struck it and killed it. Your servant has killed both the lion and the bear; this uncircumcised Philistine will be like one of them, because he has defied the armies of the living God. The Lord who rescued me from the paw of the lion and the paw of the bear will rescue me from the hand of this Philistine." Saul said to David, "Go, and the Lord be with you."

1 Samuel 17:33-37

I want to take some time to talk about the most important part of a man—his heart. Many women spend their time and effort to win the heart of a man. While their intentions may be good in most cases, the methods are all wrong. Here are some methods that will not work to get and/or keep that man.

Sex

One of the major misconceptions that women have is that if I give a man all the sex he needs, that will win his heart. This is so far from the truth. While sex may get his attention, it will not—and I repeat 'WILL NOT,' win his heart. Women must understand that sex to a man is not emotional; it is an action to prove or validate his manhood. I am not saying that he doesn't tie emotions to sex. His emphasis is placed on the goal, however, to be the best she ever had. Almost contradictory, he believes his sex game should be enough to keep her. Sex is control. This is why a man can have sex with more than one woman and have little or no emotional attachment to none of them.

Giving Him a Child

I have talked to many couples and I often hear the women say, "I gave him a child doesn't that account for something?" They thought a child would bring them closer but not so. I remember having a conversation with my ex-wife before we separated; she asked me if we had a child, would we still be together? At the time, I had no idea how to answer the question. Now, the answer I should have given, "A child will not and cannot fix a relationship or win the heart of a man!"

There are many children born as an attempt to trap or save a relationship. A generation of unwanted and mistreated children attempts to thrive with single mothers because they believed this child was the antidote to a dying relationship. Another reason most men today grew up in a house without a father is because the father is in a broken state; to stay in a situation where he has never seen a man 'step up' may make him run at first.

Taking Care of Him

Taking care of a man to win his heart can cripple him instead of function as a helpmate. A man in a broken state does not need a woman to take care of him. The problem that arises is the man gets complacent and is not held accountable for being the man he is supposed to be. This woman becomes a second mother to him instead of a helpmate. Then this same woman grows tired of doing everything and him responsible for nothing. This broken man is not going to like the shift in mindset of accountability. So he most likely will leave this woman.

Let's Talk About His Heart

The heart is the trickiest thing to obtain from a man. Men learn very early from their male influence to shield their heart, especially from a woman. Men do not deal with pain like women. We cannot take pain, especially emotional pain. When a man is emotionally broken, he begins to breakdown at the core. From my experiences, emotional pain hurts far deeper than what is visible. I can remember in my youth how abandonment, shame, and rejection from women impacted my life.

Inside the heart of a man, if he has not allowed God to heal his giant, is a bitter soar aimed at reciprocating their anger against other women. The problem is that he has suppressed this pain for years, and the moment he is reminded of a past hurt, he relives every instance all over again. Yes, when a woman hurts a man, he relives every painful situation that has ever happened to him. For example, if his father or mother yelled at him or verbally abused him, when the woman in his life yells at him, he becomes that little boy backed into the corner. He maybe afraid he is going to be hit again or even triggers a sexual assault memory. Understand that he may or may not tell another how he feels—what he sees at that moment is masked. Inside of him is a storm of emotions brewing and in some way, shape, or form, it must be dealt with.

When a man is emotionally broken, he begins to breakdown at his core. From my experiences, I can attest that for a man, it hurts far more than what is visible.

The Wounded Heart of a Man

When dealing with the heart of a man, women must realize that a man is human first like she. Men hurt just like women but are better at masking their emotions. The man's heart falls in love just as fast as females, maybe faster. He often hides it because he does not know if the woman will accept the gift he wants to give her. Musiq Soulchild has a song called, "Teach Me How to Love!" I recommend that all women in search of a man or a deeper understanding of men, listen to this song and take it seriously. There are many true statements hidden in the verses of this song all women should know.

You Were Created for My Heart

Women were created for men because we do not do alone well. Consider the situation preceding the creation of Eve. There was Adam, who had just come off of the biggest triumph of his life, and was immediately faced with the sobering reality that he was the only creation of his kind. He was lonely. God realized Adam was growing depressed because of his loneliness. Therefore, God created Adam a helpmate—Eve, to be Adam's helpmate.

When dealing with the heart of a man, women must realize that a man is human first like she. Men hurt just like women but are better at masking their emotions.

This concept still exists today. If a man is left to his own devices, he will surely self-destruct from the inside out. Knowingly or unknowingly, a man seeks a woman to help him live in this world because he cannot survive alone. Men were not created to help women...women were created to help men. This is why God chose the rib of a man when He created woman, because it is the ribs' job to protect the most delicate organs. Seemingly, without a ribcage, man is vulnerable to fatal blows. The same occurs with a woman. She is the protector, a shield from all the emotional and spiritual hurt that man may encounter. This topic is addressed in greater depth in Chapter 5 - "She Hurt Me."

CHAPTER FOUR

WHERE IS DADDY?

Then Saul dressed David in his own tunic. He put a coat of armor on him and a bronze helmet on his head. David fastened on his sword over the tunic and tried walking around, because he was not used to them. I cannot go in these," he said to Saul, "because I am not used to them." So he took them off. Then he took his staff in his hand, chose five smooth stones from the stream, put them in the pouch of his shepherd's bag and, with his sling in his hand, approached the Philistine."

1 Samuel 17:38-40

This chapter is one that impacts boys, teens, and men. As a youngling growing up without a father, I noticed a significant difference in the maturation of boys with and without fathers. I had male figures in my life, but they were not father figures. Women and the government in my opinion underestimate the importance of a father to a child. Without that connection to the father, the child cannot understand who he is. Let me explain my thoughts through telling my story:

He's Gone

I remember happy times with my father. Riding in his 18 wheeler truck, his eyes on the road, and mine affixed on playing with the CB radio. His call sign was '00 Slave,' and I was 'Slave Jr.' To me, it was the most amazing experience a 5 year old could experience. Speaking through a hand radio that transmitted sound through a little black box, that at times would talk back—super fun. Some may argue that my love with radio started then and perhaps that's true.

I recall coming off of the road with my dad. We would sit in front of the television and eat cookies (I still do this to this day). My father was the center of my world. I loved my mother but my father was my 'everything.' I looked like him, acted like him, and even dressed like him.

One day that all changed. It was a Saturday, and it was the weekend for me to stay with my dad; my father and mother did not live together. As usual on my dad's weekend, I woke up early to wait for him to come and get me. This weekend was different because my mother had married my stepfather a few days prior. My stepdad and my father had several conversations about him limiting how much my father could see me; he preferred never again. This decision by another man, to limit his rights did not sit well with him at all. He embraced his responsibility to care and raise me—no one was taking that from him.

From what I can remember, I was taken from my mother's house to the neighbor's across the street. I loved going to the Howard's house so this wasn't a problem. The neighbors had an awesome model 18-wheeler truck that reminded me of the truck my dad had. I soon fell asleep. The next thing I recalled, my uncle picked me up and took me to my grandmother's house.

As I grew older, I heard many stories about what happened that day. I believe there are 3 sides to every story—what one person thinks, what the other person thinks, and the truth. Since I will never know exactly what happened that day, the details of what I was told are this.

My stepfather for some reason—unknown to me, told my father he could not pick me up. My father began to argue with my mother and my stepfather got involved. In anger, my father gathered his brothers (my uncles) and decided that they were coming to get me regardless of my stepdad. Expecting trouble, my stepfather got his gun and my father arrived with his. There was a shoot out between them that ended with my father shot in the arm and sitting in jail. When the police attempted to understand the connection between my father and I, my mother lied and said I was not his son. As a result, I did not see him again until I was 17 years old.

As an adult I firmly believe there are many things that would not have happened to me if my father had been in my life. One critical thing that happened to me will be addressed in chapter 6 - He Touched Me, Not God.

The father plays a vital role in the lives of children, especially the son. Women should not allow their feelings about a man's worth to convince them to remove a father from the lives of their children. If the father seems to not want a relationship with the child, still try to make the child available to him. If he still does not make an effort, explain the truth to the child without embellishing. Although it may hurt, the child needs an explanation of why daddy does not want to be involved in his life. For example, my mother never told me the truth about why my father was not there for me. I developed a displacement complex, which means I knew growing up that I was different from all of my brothers and sisters. I was the only child between my father and my mother, so I grew up feeling displaced. I often felt like I did not belong. Even as an adult, I still felt as though I did not fit in with my family. Thankfully, God uses displaced people too.

I recently had a conversation with my father about my life growing up without him. I was telling him how I felt about being the only child between him and my mother, and the loneliness I felt because of it. For the majority of my life, I felt like I had no one. I told him I did not even have my mother. After the shootout, she sent me to live with my grandmother and did not have much to do with me. I really had no one but God. All my father could do was look at me, but I know empathy was felt for me.

There is no pain like a man that feels detached from his identity. With the absence of a father, a son does not know who or what he is supposed to become. I have spent my entire life looking for a father. I am 37 and I still long for that father figure that will tell me, "I'm proud of you, and I love you son!" I seek a father that will hug me when I need a hug. I have never felt love from my stepdad only obligation. Sons can feel the difference when a man really loves him and when he is only there out of obligation; this is one reason why many sons do not bond well with stepdads.

There is no pain like a man that feels detached from his identity. In the absence of a father, a son does not know who or what he is supposed to become.

Where is Daddy?

My Conversation with a Friend

I was on the phone with a good friend of mine and she wanted to ask me a question. She wanted to understand why some fathers did not want to be involved in the lives of their sons. She made it personal when she asked, "Why does he allow his wife to stand between him and his son?" At the time, I was in the process of writing this book and I had recently confronted my own father. I told her some men struggle with being a good father, if they never had a father. Again, it is extremely difficult for a man to be a great father without an example. What has happened in the Black community and has permeated through America is *Collective Identity. Collective Identity* is the phenomenon where an individual identifies him or herself with the attributes of a collective group, likely because there is no other identifying factor available. Communities over time have made it socially normal for a father to be absent. There is a system created that supports absenteeism of a father in the home.

Sons can feel the difference when a man really loves him and when he is only there out of obligation; this is one reason why many sons do not bond well with stepfathers.

Many times, I have heard men say, "If she is not with me, then I don't want to have anything to do with the child." This type of thinking has sparked a negative movement among men, which makes the mother's of these children bitter, and enables them to teach hatred to the children. We must understand that this problem did not start with this generation; it started with slavery for blacks and with others, families who believed the man wasn't good enough for their daughter.

Let us explore. If we take a poll using women and ask them who taught them how do be a woman, they would most likely say their mothers, grandmothers, sisters, or aunts. The poll with men is a little different. Based on social group, race, and economical status, the answers will vary. Populations of men have no positive role models to encourage him in healthy habits. Pimps, drug dealers, and criminals through music and other means, to the contrary encourage many young men.

My heart breaks because I realize how bad of a state we are in as Americans. I must put some emphasis on the Black community to say, statistical data from the census has revealed minimal growth from 2008 to 2010. This community compared to others, has had stagnated growth and it is in my opinion because the family structure is askew. Fathers need to take their place and women need to allow them to stand.

Chapter Five

She hurt Me

So the Philistine came, and began drawing near to David, and the man who bore the shield went before him. And when the Philistine looked about and saw David, he disdained him; for he was only a youth, ruddy and good- looking. So the Philistine said to David, "Am I a dog, that you come to me with sticks?" And the Philistine cursed David by his gods. And the Philistine said to David, "Come to me, and I will give your flesh to the birds of the air and the beasts of the field!" Then David said to the Philistine, "You come to me with a sword, with a spear, and with a javelin. But I come to you in the name of the Lord of hosts, the God of the armies of Israel, whom you have defied.

1 Samuel 1:41-45

It is amazing to me the amount of details a man's mind can remember on situations that have hurt him. I have to admit that men process pain much differently than women. Most men have been taught to not be vulnerable to pain. The truth, this is unachievable request. Men learn to pretend they are not hurt to appear to keep up with this facade.

The reason I titled this chapter "She Hurt Me" is because there is no other pain like the pain that comes from a woman. As a man who has been hurt many times by women, I can testify it is pain like no other. I can remember as a teenager when my first relationship went bad; it literally felt like a 100-pound gorilla was sitting on my chest. The pain of heartbreak is so strong because nothing cures it but time. Please understand, when I speak of pain from a woman, I am not only referring to romantic relationships but also those with family members; mother, sister, aunt, etc. All emotional pain from a woman plays a part in the way he processes interactions—romantically or otherwise, with women.

Pain from a Mother

There were two very small, yet painful situations that shaped the way I viewed women and how I treated them. The first situation occurred when I was 8 years old. I was lying across the bed at my grandmother's house when I heard my grandmother come in from the store. I was always very close to my grandmother and I would often run to her and give her a kiss. On this particular day, something changed in the manner in which my grandmother greeted me. I ran to her to give her my usual kiss and for some reason, she pushed me away and told me, "Go sit down somewhere!"

This rejection hurt my heart because I didn't understand what I did for her to push me away. I later discovered her new boyfriend didn't like any of her grandchildren, especially me her presumed favorite. My grandmother was the last family I had. My father was in jail, my mother left me for her new family, and now my grandmother is gone too. I believe lots of men are snatched from their support system and are unsure how to process the rejection.

Men fear rejection and loneliness more than we care to admit. The most common way a man hides his fear is by becoming emotionally detached. Detached to where people coming and going is not a shock because in his mind he has already planned your exit.

The second situation that shaped my life was when I was 11. In school I had some bad behavior issues. I admit I was a troubled students at times—but not every time. On this particular day, I was not doing anything wrong but I was accused. A teacher said that I was behind the school drinking with friends. I remember standing next to my coach, watching the kids go behind the building to drink—I knew they would get busted. I was shock to find I was called into the principal's office, but was sure I would quickly be excused.

The principal began to interrogate the students asking each person about their whereabouts. All the students said I wasn't present. My coach also came into the office to validate my story that satisfied the principal but didn't convince my mother. I was facing expulsion for the remainder of the year because of a lie. I pleaded with my mother telling, "I didn't do it. I was nowhere around when they were drinking."

I was off the hook for expulsion but I felt persecuted by my mother. After the ordeal she sent me to live with my grandmother. I felt she planned to get rid of me and was waiting for an opportunity. I was the black sheep of the family and perhaps I reminded her, him, of what they did to my father.

The worst pain I felt in my young life was facing the realization my mother did not want me anymore. At that point, I made a life altering decision that I would go through life not needing anything or anyone. I admit it was when I decided to live with this toxic mindset, my life began a downward spiral.

The Toxic Mindset

Men can suffer from toxic mindsets that were created from childhood hurt. There is no logical thought process strong enough to offset the mindset developed when a child. In other words, most men that suffer from toxic mindsets were too immature to process pain correctly. It is a challenge for a man to direct his life emotionally, financially, and spiritually amidst a toxic mindset. In mindset, there is a such thing of a boy trapped in a man's body.

There is no logical thought process strong enough to offset the mindset developed when a child

Addressing a toxic mindset with a man is a delicate conversation. Most men don't like to acknowledge pain, especially emotional pain because it may appear as weakness. The danger of a toxic mindset is not realized until it is challenged. This challenge at first onset may appear to challenge his manhood.

Men that are suffering from toxic mindsets have identified themselves with their mindsets. This means that anything that challenges his mindset is a enemy to his manhood. This enemy must be destroyed before any damage can be done. I did not get rid of my toxic mindset until I realized how it limited my progression to live better. It took me to 'hit rock bottom' before I began to actively seek help.

There are two common ways people change their mindset. Men exchange their mindset for that of Christ; meaning they acknowledge their shortcomings and the power in Jesus to pull them through. The second, they conduct a self-assessment and try to reverse bad decisions for a new result. It is my opinion, but all toxic mindsets require supernatural help that comes from God. Every man that has a toxic mindset must be delivered and healed from his past hurts. Through this process you become the man God created you to be.

Pain from a Relationship

"There is no pain like the pain from a broken heart" is what my father told me when I realized my first wife did not love me anymore. Our marriage was beyond repair and had reached an end. Of all the pain a man can endure, it is the change of a woman's heart that is the most destructive. It is the nature of most men, to seek out a woman that makes a great wife. The problem is when we open ourselves to love and the woman cast away our heart. This kills a man's giant.

When a man loves, he does not just give his heart, but he also gives apart of his essence. He shares his hopes, dreams, fears, strengths, weaknesses, and shortcomings and hopes she remains. It is with this unconditional giving that he fears getting hurt. This is why it is so hard for most men to open up and give all of themselves, because they fear vulnerability.

Why Men Cheat

In counseling, I hear numerous clients ask me, "Why do men cheat?" There is no concrete reason;

however, one of the most common reasons is to protect himself. I know this concept does not make any sense to women but work with me. In a man's mind by my findings, for him to feel protected in a relationship with a woman he loves, he must find a way to devalue her. He can devalue her by verbal, physical, or emotional abuse. The most common way is to cheat on her with another woman who "so-call" gives him what he is not getting from her. Now this happens solely within the man's mind and has nothing to do with his heart. So yes, a man can be in love with a woman and still cheat on her. The reason behind the cheating is not for an emotional connection as he has that already at home; however, he cheats to have a second option in case the woman he is with decides she wants to walk away. It may not appear logical or correct but that is his thinking.

It has also been previously mentioned that when a man's giant is killed, it restores as a hybrid giant that now hates the thing that killed it. Therefore, if a woman killed the man's giant, it is more likely he will become predator and not a lover. If men were interviewed on why they treat women badly, I promise the main reason will be because of his past hurt by another woman.

Why it Hurts So Bad

When I was about 17, I received a revelation from God concerning what a woman is to a man...not just spiritually, but naturally as well. The story of Adam and Eve is well known, and describes how God took a rib from Adam to create Eve. I asked God one day, "Why did you take a rib from man to make woman?" He then asked me, "What does a rib do in the natural sense?" I replied, "It protects the vital organs from being punctured, because if any of these organs are harmed, man will die." He said to me, "Woman was created from the rib of a man because she was created to protect the delicate and vulnerable parts of man." Seemingly, a woman is the emotional protector of a man. The conflict occurs when the one created to protect becomes the reason of emotionally distress. It is this distress that most men are not prepared to handle.

Communication is Key

In order for men to free themselves from the emotional pain from any relationship, he must be open to communicate. He must be willing to let go of any toxic mindsets and not fear progress. The people in his life must also be patient for him to reveal the root of the problem, protect his trust, and if able help him through it. Finally, all parties involved must be committed to making sure the man is held accountable for continuing through the process. (If you have the workbook I encourage you to go through section 5 at this time.)

CHAPTER SIX

HE TOUCHED ME (NOT GOD)

This day the Lord will deliver you into my hand,
and I will strike you and take your head from you.
And this day I will give the carcasses of the camp of
the Philistines to the birds of the air and the wild
beasts of the earth, that all the earth may know that
there is a God in Israel. Then all this assembly shall
know that the Lord does not save with sword and
spear; for the battle is the Lord's, and He will give
you into our hands."

1 Samuel 1:46-47

This chapter is based on a sensitive subject and is intended to help other males receive healing—like I did from molestation (sex abuse) and homosexuality. I am a survivor because many men who have suffered sexual abuse still walk around as victims. I cannot describe the catastrophic effects of sexual abuse on a young man. Many men change their natural liking for a woman for a man because of a choice another person made that violated them. Statistics reveal that 1 out of 6 men have been sexually assaulted before the age of 18 (U.S. Center for Disease Control). This is probably a low estimate because it does not include noncontact experiences.

Sexual Abuse is described as unwanted sexual contact involving force, threats, or a large age difference between the child and the other person (which involves a big power differential and exploitation).

There are many factors that impact how victims handle abuse. The frequency, the number of years, who was involved, if you reported it, and if so, what was the response received. As men we can no longer look at physical abuse as something that can be 'swept under the rug.' Sexual abuse does not make a man weak. It is also a topic that should not be stricken from speech. This is the type of mindset that is common makes men not want to deal with abuse.

Many men live in a private 'hell.' They are screaming out in silence praying that someone will hear and save. There are too many men that suppress or deny that they were sexual abused. Unfortunately, they do not realize that they are living with physical and emotional scars that can't heal until they are first addressed.

I know about this hell because I once lived in it. I will do my best to outline the healing processes that the Lord shared with me that brought me to healing and deliverance; but first I want to share a few bits of knowledge.

The Numbers

- A 2005 study conducted by the U.S. Centers for Disease Control, on San Diego Kaiser Permanente HMO members, reported that 16% of males were sexually abused by the age of 18.
- A 2003 national study of U.S. adults reported that 14.2% of men were sexually abused before the age of 18.
- A 1998 study researched male childhood sexual abuse and concluded that reporting was, "... under-reported, under-recognized, and under-treated."
- A 1996 study of male university students in Boston reported 18% of men were sexually abused before the age of 16.

- A 1990 national study of U.S. adults reported that 16% of men were sexually abused before the age of 18.

Although these numbers are startling and depressing, it is believed that these numbers are a gross underestimation of actual numbers. Males are less likely to disclose or discuss that they have been physically abused compared to females. Only 16% of men with documented histories of sexual abuse (by social service agencies which tend to be the most serious) considered themselves to have been sexually abused, compared to 64% of women with documented histories in the same study.

It has become increasingly important to investigate the sexual abuse of our young men because they grow up to become men with very serious mental health issues. Statistics show that men that have been sexually abused as children, suffer from a wide range of mental health issues such as—but not limited to, symptoms of post- traumatic stress disorder and depression. Many of them turn to a life of alcoholism and drug abuse as a means of coping with the emotional scars. They suffer from suicidal thoughts commonly as well.

Sadly, many have attempted suicide some unfortunately being successful. We also find intimacy issues with men that have been sexually abused as children. It is these apparent problems that make it hard for some men to have successful relationships with the opposite sex. Finally, sexual abuse causes men to experience underachievement at school and at work. They grow to accept dysfunction and limitations. The macho mindset doesn't help men rebound from such events either.

Finally, sexual abuse causes men to experience underachievement at school and at work. They grow to accept dysfunction and limitations.

My Story

Before I share my story, I will disclose the reason why I am so willing to share it with the world. I can remember having a conversation with Pastor Ida in Baton Rouge, Louisiana, approximately 12 years ago. She said to me,

"When you can openly talk about what happened and you don't go back into a deep depression. You don't relive the experience or when you discuss the experience your thoughts don't breed hatred. When your thoughts go into a place of love and you genuinely want to see the abusers saved and forgiven--that's when you are ready to move to share your testimony with the world. Your testimony of healing, deliverance can help someone else make it through."

I can truly say that I am ready to share my story with the world in hopes that it helps someone who feels like there is no more hope. I pray you realize you (he) do not have to live in a private hell any longer. God can help you (or him) the same way he has helped me.

The First Time

It was around 2004. I was scheduled to speak at the Pastor's Appreciation at a church in Houston, Texas and I was having what I used to call an *emotional episode.* I dreamt about the sexual abuse in my youth, and I relived the experience all over again. I had these dreams periodically and would be emotionally crippled until I was able to shake the feeling and move on. This Sunday morning I had to deliver a message on hope when I felt hopeless. I would often ask God, "How can I preach life when I am dying inside?"

I remember this day as if it were yesterday, because it was the day I realized I had power. I do not know how I got through that sermon without breaking down and losing it, but God got me through it. Towards the end of the message and just before the Alter Call, the Lord instructed me to tell my testimony. Since everything was fresh on my mind from my night's dream. I told my story. How it happened and who did it. When I looked up, there was not a dry eye in the place. Shortly after, the Altar was full of people—men and women alike, wanting me to pray for their strength and deliverance.

One lady in particular stood out amongst the rest. She told me after church she had planned to commit suicide because she felt alone. She experienced sexual and emotional abuse, and felt no one could understand. After hearing me tell my story she trusted God to heal her and give her strength to persevere. She received Jesus as her Lord and Savior, and was healed from emotional scars since that day.

The Saturday That Changed My Life

It was a day in October of 1984 when I received a new bike. I was riding with 3 other people in a newly developed neighborhood where we recently moved into a house. We were riding on a trail in a wooded area with a stream on the far backside. As I cautiously approached the stream, I was yanked from my bike to the ground. While stunned from hitting the ground, my shorts were snatched off and the two younger boys held me down. The oldest of the three raped me and when he finishes the other two took their turns. I remember hearing my scream, but after a while I just laid there numb and lifeless.

After they were done, I was told that if I told anyone what happened, they would kill me and my mother. I must have laid there torn and bleeding in the grass for about an hour. My innocence ripped from me, pain striking through my body with each passing moment. This was the Saturday that forever changed my life.

I wish I could say that the abuse stopped here, but it did not. The abuse continued until I was 13 years old and moved with my grandmother. At times, I feel that my mother sent me to live with my grandmother because she knew what was happening. She, perhaps, did not want to risk losing her new marriage, so she sent me away. She swept it 'under the rug' and I tried to as well. I was unsuccessful and I was tormented—haunted by what happened to me. It was not until the Lord showed me that the root of my problem was with my mother, father, God, and myself. I was the picture of a young man that was molested as a child and I lashed out until Jesus saved me.

My Inner Battle

In addition to all of the emotional and psychological issues, the hardest battle was the spiritual ones. Because of the rape, until the age of 17, I struggled with my sexuality. I never willfully had sex with a man but the door was open for to that spirit. My thoughts became so bad, I dreamt about being a female to cope. I was living an alternate life in my mind. The dreams I was having was trying to manifest themselves into my natural life. Although I was in active ministry, no one knew of my silent inner hell. I repeatedly prayed and fasted to be free. On many occasions I tried to kill myself, but it was God's will I was unsuccessful. Nothing worked. I just wanted to end it all.

Amazingly, one night I dreamt that an angel and a demon were fighting for me. In the dream, the angel defeated the demon, and the demon blew up before my eyes. I could feel the explosion as if it really happened. When I woke up, I was totally free from all feminine mannerisms and characteristics. I felt renewed and masculine. To this day, I do not have any residual effects of feeling womanly, and others are astonished to know that I ever struggled with my sexuality.

Although I was set free from the effeminate effects, I developed another dangerous problem; promiscuous. This was my way to prove to myself I was not gay. I went out and had sex with every woman I could find. I became so indiscriminate that I did not even know why I was having so much sex; it was as if I was a slave to a need that was never quenched.

It is believed that men who have been molested will travel down one of two paths—homosexuality or promiscuity. I became the latter of the two. It was not until I wanted to become different that a change occurred. Vividly speaking, "No matter what extreme you find yourself, God has the power to set you free, but you have to want it. Dedication to not make excuses but necessary changes becomes paramount."

The Mind of the Victim

A victim has very unstable thoughts. I recall being molested day-after-day by the same people, and my mind became cluttered. I often felt that if I was going to be treated like a girl, then I might as well become one. What was really happening to me is that the giant in me was dying and accepting the abuse as normal. This is not a place easily escaped. To get to this point of accepting abnormal activity as normal, a constant chipping away of a man's self-esteem, manhood, and desire has to happen. This place is accompanied by much pain and despair. The earlier this takes place in a man's life, the seemingly more difficult it is to desire and believe in change. Pain and suffering can become a part of his personality. This makes the man feel that he is not worthy of love. He is a damaged good. No one could possibly love him if they knew what happened to him.

What was really happening to me is that the giant in me was dying and accepting that this was my life. This is not a place easily escaped. This place comes through the constant chipping away of a man's self-esteem, manhood, and desire to live.

When a man succumbs to homosexuality after being molested as a child, it is the reaction of his giant dying. He then succumbs to the pain that he cannot deal with. He becomes what his molester made him become during the act of sexual abuse. It becomes easier for him to yield to the pain than fight against it.

This person can be delivered, make no doubt about it; if he wants it. It is my belief that most men who struggle with homosexuality because of molestation really do not want to live this way. These men just struggle to be free from the pain and there is help. This does not mean those who choose homosexuality cannot be delivered; they can too. God is able to save all that put their faith and trust in Him. He is mighty to save.

The Mind of the Victor

In the beginning of the chapter, I spoke of me being a survivor of sexual abuse and not a victim of sexual abuse. Society persuades men to believe that they will always be a victim, instead of telling men that the essence of who they are shows that they are fighters. I stand today as a free man of any residual effects of sexual abuse. I am happily married with a wonderful family of 6 kids. I am a well-adjusted adult that is the Lead Pastor of The Healing Place in Texas. I have a successful loving relationship without devaluing my wife. I am an individual who speaks to male youth and men about being free from the effects of sexual abuse, homosexual and transgender thoughts, or alternative lifestyles. I am here to proclaim that if God can do it for me, He can do it for anyone.

The Healing Process

The process of healing from sexual abuse can be a long and emotionally-taxing process. There are 3 main stages. It is in understanding the healing stages that we can effectively help someone navigate through the process. It also should be noted, if after the incident the healing process begins, toxic mindsets can be offset.

The Victim Stage

When the event happens, the person becomes a victim of sexual abuse. During this time, the person searches for some type of help to deal with the negative emotions. Bitterness can also creep in and attempt to torment.

It also should be noted, if after the incident the healing process begins, toxic mindsets can be offset.

Survivor Stage

After the initial shock of the event the person begins to experience fight or flight. In most cases the man decides to fight back with toxic mindsets. This stage is called the Survivor stage. This is when the person does everything they can do to survive.

Overcomer Stage

Once a person has reached the survivor stage, there comes a point where the individual realizes that there is more to life than just surviving. Those who want to experience healing and are dedicated to becoming healed pass this stage. When one becomes an overcomer, it is then that he is ready to share his testimony with the world. He is also able to become a beacon of proof that others can complete the healing process. Overcomers do not live life with the residual effects of sexual abuse because they are delivered.

Special Message

This message is for my brothers that are still struggling with their sexuality because they were abused. I know how it feels as I have been in that same place. I understand the pain and the brokenness that one must feel. The endless waves of emotions and thoughts that cannot be shared with others, because they will not understand, I understand. I know what it feels like to think you are damaged goods and undeserving of anyone's love. Many feel as though they are not even worthy of God's love. I stand strong and am willing to walk through this with you. God did it for me and can do it for you.

CHAPTER SEVEN

HOW TO RAISE THE GIANT IN A MAN

The factors that can kill a giant in a man have been previously discussed, so now let us explore what can raise a giant in a man. There is only one real way that a man's giant can be raised. This way is by the Power of God through Jesus; however, there are some necessary steps that need to take place in order for deliverance to be complete. In this chapter, we will discuss the steps that will ensure that the wounded man's giant is raised and is healthy once again.

It is imperative to follow specific steps when raising a man's giant because the recovery status is based upon the entire process being done correctly. Many times we try to take someone through a deliverance process without understanding what the person is dealing with or have. This is why deliverance is short-lived at best, and we see people back in those same situations. We must understand that this is a deliverance process and must not be entered into lightly, because an unsuccessful deliverance process will cause more harm than good.

Step One

The first step in any deliverance process is bringing the person to a place of realizing that he is in need of deliverance. It is very difficult to raise the giant in a man if he does not know his giant is dead or is dying. In most cases, it is a devastating, or life-altering event that forces the man to face his problem. Rarely does a man just say, "I am in need of help." Most cases it takes the people closest to him to point out his needs. It is at this point the woman in his life becomes an active part in his deliverance process. I must emphasize this is when the most demonic opposition is present. The enemy does not want him to be delivered and will cause many distractions to prohibit change.

False deliverance

It is important that when taking a man through this process, we pay close attention for signs of false deliverance. False deliverance comes before true deliverance takes place. A spirit of deception enters and offers the impression that deliverance has taken place and the contrary is true. What has actually occurred is a spirit of deception from the enemy has come to block the man's deliverance. He will appear to be delivered, until the very thing that killed his giant tests his deliverance. It is imperative that when tested, the strength to avoid the pitfall comes from God and not the man or his help. If it is from the help, he will most likely fail and become worst.

The deliverance process should not be started or attempted by someone who is not trained in the deliverance process. Too many times, untrained and immature Christians try to take someone through the deliverance process and cause more damage than healing. An individual must be prepared spiritually to successfully take someone through the deliverance process.

To identify false deliverance, the person administering the process must have keen spiritual discernment. I state this because in most cases, there is no second chance to speak to the spirit of deception before it takes root. It will be the administrator's responsibility to identify the spirit that is at work, and make the proper adjustments while in the deliverance process.

In some cases, it will be required for the administrator to speak to the spirit of deception.

This must be done carefully and under the guidance of the Holy Spirit. If this is done incorrectly, it can cause the man to feel like he is being attacked instead of helped; thus causing him to become guarded and unreceptive to the deliverance that the Holy Spirit offers. Once the spirit of deception has come in and is trying to cause a false deliverance to happen, the Holy Spirit must order and direct the steps for the administrator.

To bring a man to realize he needs deliverance is a 'slippery slope' and must not be taken lightly; especially if he has not ready to receive deliverance. He has to be at the stage where he realizes he is inadequate, is in need of help, and wants the prayers of others.

It is important to not be fooled by the man attempting to push everyone away. It is only his flesh creating a lying reality to protect him against true deliverance. Again, it is critical to fast and pray. Matt.17:21: "But this kind does not go out except by prayer and fasting." We cannot give up but must maintain the commitment to see the man made whole.

To bring a man to realize he needs deliverance is a 'slippery slope' and must not be taken lightly; especially if he has not ready to receive deliverance.

Step Two

73

After helping the man to realize deliverance is needed, step two is to pinpoint the problem that caused his giant to be killed. In my opinion, this is the most important part of the process because it is the step that sets-up the man for continued spiritual success. This is the time when he will need strong spiritual help and guidance. It will take a trained eye to walk him through the process of identifying the root of his issues. One must understand that this is a hard process. It is hard because he must now face the painful time(s) in his life that he most likely suppressed. It is important during this time to pray against the spirit of depression because that is the next spirit sent by the enemy.

Spiritual Deflection

One of the major hindrances during this step is what I refer to as *spiritual deflection*. Spiritual deflection is when the man deflects to a lesser, painful issue that is easier for him to deal with instead of dealing with the root. This occurs when the main issue is confronted and is too painful, or he has created a stronghold in his mind to protect himself from the pain associated with the issue.

Another key element is **self-constructed strongholds**. Self-constructed strongholds are strongholds that have been set up to protect the persons' soul from the pain of the issue he is trying to suppress. This stronghold is by far the hardest to penetrate because the person views it as a protection rather than the cause. Because the man believes the

74

stronghold helps, he will do whatever it takes to protect it and no matter the cost.

The major problem with this particular type of stronghold is that it becomes a part of that persons' personality. It imbeds itself into the psyche of the person so much so that it becomes a mindset and a way of processing cognitive information. When facing this type of stronghold, one must get the person to realize that the issue he is protecting is hurting him in subtle ways. The atmosphere during this stage must be conducive to spiritual and emotional healing. To be such, judgment must not be present. It is impossible to help someone deal with a painful issue if he has not ascertained the issue.

One must be careful when helping a person during this time, because there can be no true deliverance without getting rid of the issue. It is important that one not only identifies the issue, but also states and addresses the root issue.

Step Three

The next step in the process is ***spiritual cleansing***. At this phase, there is no turning back— deliverance must take place because the real issue has been exposed.

Spiritual Cleansing is when the person is taken though the process of expelling every spiritual force that has been legally let in due to the self-

constructed strongholds and areas of un-
forgiveness that exist within the soul.

It is important to fully allow the Holy Spirit to cleanse the soul of the person before the deliverance process is complete. Make sure one does not stop the deliverance process before it is completed, because this will open the door for more demonic activity.

Jesus found him in the Temple and told him, "Look! You have become well. Stop sinning or something worse may happen to you." John 5:14.

Forgiveness is Key

It is vital that the man going through the deliverance process forgives those who have hurt him or caused the issue that has wreaked havoc in his life. This is one of those times when he and the one administering must be 'prayed up' because this is not for the person that hurt him—it is for him to be free. If the person that is to be forgiven is alive, the man must seek out that person face-to-face. He must tell the individual that he forgives him/her, and in turn asks for forgiveness for holding un-forgiveness toward the person in his heart.

Make sure one does not stop the deliverance process before it is completed, because this will open the door for more demonic activity.

The man must also be prepared for the person who he forgives to react poorly to the conversation of forgiveness. The inability to forgive will stop the deliverance process before it has a chance to take place. Forgiveness is one of the most lethal weapons of the enemy, because it is in direct disobedience to the Word and Will of God.

"For if you forgive others for their transgressions, your heavenly Father will also forgive you. 15 But if you do not forgive others, then your Father will not forgive your transgressions" (Matt. 6:14-15).

If the person or people that are to be forgiven are unavailable for a face-to-face meeting, the man must picture the person in front of him while stating that he forgives; as well as ask God for forgiveness for holding un-forgiveness. The man must state the means in which he releases whoever he pictures before him, from any debt and ill feelings, and walk away from the picture while leaving the pain behind. This process can be done all at once or multiple times—whatever is more effective for the man that is seeking deliverance.

My final note on forgiveness is that the person in seeking deliverance must ask the Father to forgive the man for holding un-forgiveness in order to truly be set free. Un-forgiveness is a sin and must be presented to the Father through Jesus for proper disposal and cleansing. This is a vital step in the process and must be explained because many people struggle with forgiving someone that has brought them emotional and even spiritual harm. In truth, the Lord requires us to forgive in order for us to be forgiven, which is the foundation of true deliverance.

Denounce the Pain

It is important when going through the deliverance process; the man denounces the pain of the situation or person that caused his giant to be killed. It is during this time that he can become free of demonic forces that gained legal access to his life through un-forgiveness. It is critical to verbally state the feelings, mindsets, and/or sinful activity that need to be denounced. This is needed in order to serve notice to the spiritual forces that have taken residence within the strongholds that have been set-up either by the person or demonic forces that seek to hide within the man's soul.

For example, if one of the toxic behaviors is sexual immorality, the man should decree and declare that,

"I'm speaking to the spirit of perversion--I command you to leave my life with all of the residual effects of you taking up residence in my life. I declare this by the Power of the Holy Ghost that lives in me, and gives me power over all demonic forces. Those that are within me and outside of me trying to gain access to my life. Lord, I thank you that I am free and will never deal with this spirit again. In Jesus' Name Amen."

It is vital that the person seeking deliverance allows the Holy Spirit to guide him through this process, especially when expelling all demonic forces that are identified by the Holy Spirit.

Conclusion

The process of raising the giant in a man is a intense, but necessary process that cannot be taken lightly. It is in this process that the man is set free from all the demonic forces that have held him captive; and made him unable to mature spiritually. It is essential to note that after the raising of his giant, the demonic forces be replaced with the presence of God in order to prevent demonic activity from returning seven times greater. If this process is not abandoned but seen through to the end, the man will have a new and exciting life that is ready and free from all residual effects of past situations, circumstances, and relationships.

CHAPTER EIGHT

CONNECTING WITH THE GOD NATURE WITHIN

Now the men of Israel and Judah arose and shouted, and pursued the Philistines as far as the entrance of the valley[a] and to the gates of Ekron. And the wounded of the Philistines fell along the road to Shaaraim, even as far as Gath and Ekron. 53 Then the children of Israel returned from chasing the Philistines, and they plundered their tents. 54 And David took the head of the Philistine and brought it to Jerusalem, but he put his armor in his tent.

1 Samuel 1:52-54

I am so excited about writing this chapter because this is not only for men, but also for all who are saved and want to connect with the greater part of that man. The truth is most of us that are saved have no idea of the power that lives within us. The Bible says in 1 John 4:4, "You are of God, little children, and I have overcame them, because He who is in you is greater than he who is in the world." It is this greater person that is within us that gives us the power to do some amazing things. The problem is that many of us limit ourselves by thinking we are the person with the same limitations we had before we got saved. Philippians 4:13 states, "I can do all things through Christ who strengthens me." This is by far the greatest indicator of the power that lives within the true believer in Christ.

The Problem

When we get saved, no one tells us what really happens. We create unrealistic expectations and place limitations on God when He is limitless. Question: Did God become any less God when He filled man with His Spirit? The answer is "No." It is impossible for a limitless God to have limits. God requires us to come up to His expectation. The Bible says in Leviticus 11:44, "For **I am** the Lord your God. You shall therefore consecrate yourselves, and you shall be **holy**; for **I am holy."** Holiness has been viewed as a chore in the modern church when in actuality, we have been made a new creature. The nature of the new creature, is to be and desire holiness as found in 2 Corinthians 5:17,

"Therefore, if anyone *is* in Christ, *he is* a **new** creation; old things have passed away; behold, all things have become **new**."

Philippians 4:13 states, "I can do all things through Christ who strengthens me." This is by far the greatest indicator of the power that lives within the true believer in Christ.

Although we look the same on the outside, our souls and spirits have been created anew. All we have to do is yield to the newness given to us when Christ comes to live within us. Gal. 2:20 says, "I have been crucified with Christ; it is no longer I who live, but Christ lives in me; and the *life* which I now live in the flesh, I live by faith in the Son of God, who loved me and gave Himself for me."

If our minds are not renewed to the distinctive mindset of salvation, we will constantly be slaved to the old man oblivious we were made anew. The enemy will try to block us from the knowledge of who we are in Christ, but do not let him win.

The God Nature Revealed

The key to 'The God Nature' is found in 2 Peter 1:4, "By which have been given to us exceedingly great and precious promises, that through these you may be partakers of the **divine (GOD) nature**, having escaped the corruption *that is* in the world through lust." With this nature comes Power, Authority, and the ability to overcome all things and live a holy life without sin or limitation. I understand that this is a huge statement, but once we submit ourselves to 'The God Nature,' we can live a holy life without sin and limitations. No one has to be held captive to sin.

If our minds are not renewed to the distinctive mindset of salvation, we will constantly be slaved to the old man oblivious we were made anew.

Let us journey through the process in which the Lord took me when He first explained The God Nature to me. It starts in First John the first chapter. I will highlight the Scriptures in this passage and explain as the Father explained it to me:

In the beginning was the Word, and the Word was with God, and the Word was God.

- The word is eternal and was with God in the beginning of all things, and is still with God now, and through this eternal connection, we have access to all things eternal. When I say all things eternal, I mean eternal power, authority, and knowledge.
- Because of The Word that lives in us, we are seated in heavenly places with God (eternal and powerful **Ephesians 1:20**). **He was in the beginning with God. All things were made through Him, and without Him nothing was made that was made.**

- Because all things were made by him, the Him that lives in us, we have access to the person that created all things. Not from a distance, but inside of us at this very moment.
- The *He* that lives in us brings life and gives us the ability to bring life to all things in which we come in contact. That is why there should never be a problem for us to operate in divine healing because the healer lives within us. This is why it is so easy for me to operate in the miraculous, because I understand who lives in me. I understand my position and am a vessel not the main attraction.

And the light shines in the darkness, and the darkness did not comprehend it.

- Because He was such an agent of social change, so shall those be He lives within. That is why the Bible says in **Psalm 97:10,** "Let those who love the LORD hate evil, for He guards the lives of His faithful ones and delivers them from the hand of the wicked."
- Because He that lives in us was so hated by the world and the religious community when He walked the earth, why should we be treated any differently? Not only will the world hate us and misunderstand us, but also those within the church that is not really connected to Him. Those that are living a

life not worthy of His calling will hate us as well.

- Because of this, most do not fit in with the world or the church; they only fit in with The Kingdom.

But for those who have received Him, to them, God gave them power to become the Son of God, even to them that believe on His name:

- Because of our surrender, we were given the power to become The Sons of God. Now we have the ability to manifest our son-ship in every situation, circumstance, and relationship we find ourselves in.
- Because we are now Sons, creation is looking and waiting on us to give it directive on what to do in the earth realm. **Romans 8:19** declares that, "For the creation eagerly waits with anticipation for God's sons to be revealed."
- It is time for the Sons to wake up and be revealed.

Which were born, not of blood, nor of the will of the flesh, nor of the will of man, but of God.

- Because He made us Sons, we have no connection to the flesh, because we were not called and born after the flesh. We are after the Spirit. This is why nothing we do in the flesh works out because we are no longer a part of that system. Success in this realm will dwindle.

- Although our parents decided to come together and make us, it was the divine will and decision of the Father that we were born. One day we will become a Son and do great works for the Kingdom. **Jeremiah 1:5,** "Before I formed you in the womb, I knew you, before you were born I set you apart; I appointed you as a prophet to the nations."

And the word was made flesh, and dwelt among us, (and we beheld his glory, the glory as of the only begotten of the Father,) full of grace and truth.

- Because He that lives within us lived in the flesh victoriously, naturally, we should live victoriously as well.
- Because of Him, we have the ability to take dominion over every demonic force that we think has control over our life. We can take dominion and live the life the Lord promised.

A Natural Representation of What Happens

The easiest way to describe what happens to us when we reach and cross the demarcation point of salvation. It is like when a caterpillar becomes a butterfly. The butterfly goes into a cocoon as an ugly worm with all of its limitations and venerability that comes with being a worm. Like myself, I was a wretched soul, broken with no direction, in need of a serious life change. I felt like I was damaged goods and nobody wanted me. Then I got saved and this former worm became the beautiful butterfly. I became a new creation that does not look back to my former self to dictate my future. I can't go back to what I was because I have been changed; my character is anew. I don't crawl to get around but I fly.

It's a Mind Thing

The Bible says in **Philippians 2:5,** "Let this mind be in you, which was also in Christ Jesus." It is not the issue of whether we have been recreated as a creature whose core nature is that of holiness and power; it is the issue of whether we believe or know it. The enemy's job is to do his best to keep us ignorant of the power we possess inside. Because we do not know it, he demolishes our life by stealing from us, killing us with sinful desire, and having us to believe that it is ok to live in this way. Finally, he destroys any chance of us reaching the full potential that the Father has destined for us.

In order to connect with 'The God Nature' inside, one must do this 3-step process that the Lord took me through:

1. One must unlearn and denounce all erroneous teaching that one he/she received throughout life as it relates to holy living.

   One cannot put old and flawed teaching on top of fresh revelation. The old teaching will war against the fresh revelation. If he/she is not rooted and grounded in the Word, he/she runs the risk of the new revelation being expelled. One must be open to receive a new way to approach salvation and the new creation.

2. Allow the 'Mind' of Christ to become the mindset—allowing all cognitive processes to be processed through.

The Mind of Christ is the Word because He is the Word made flesh. The only way to get the Mind of Christ is to be on a steady diet of the Word. We should try to spend at least 2 hours per day with God in the following manner:

30 Min = Reading the word.

30 Min = Praying targeted prayers (prayers prayed for a certain purpose using the Word as a catalyst to affect change.) (Isaiah 55:11)

30 Min = Speaking in tongues/praying in our prayer language. (Jude 1:20)

30 Min = Listening and writing the directives and spiritual insight given by the Father.

3. Accept who you are. Christ lives in you and He decides from this day forward what you are to accept. Anything less than the heritage given by God will not do.

Begin immediately to think and act as the Son of God. This means when it comes to our lifestyle, cut off all things that are contrary to what the Mind of Christ says is an acceptable way of living.

Manifest our sonship in every area of your life. From your finances to marriage, we should always be seen as the Son of God. If you are not convinced, continue to proclaim it over your life until it soaks in.

Conclusion

This is only a snippet of what the Lord showed me about 'The God Nature' that lives inside of us. It hurts to know that so many people who have accepted Christ, have been given so much power, and are living a life far below God's standard. I pray that this chapter gives men and women alike, a reason to begin the internal conversations of deeper thoughts—thoughts which focus on the core of our being. Put down the crutches of religion that teaches us what it takes to be saved! If you dismiss this knowledge, by not accepting the Holy Spirit, be prepared to continue to live life defeated.

One thing for certain, we must understand that reading truth, we are now accountable. For those who want to know more about 'The God Nature,' stay tuned to my next book, "Be Ye Mature"—A Practical Guide to Living The God Nature.

ABOUT THE AUTHOR

Dr. Cedric White was born on August 6, 1974 in Baton Rouge, Louisiana. He is the founder of The Healing Place located in Dallas Texas and Dr. Cedric White Ministries. Dr. Cedric White has dedicated his life to serving God and humanity. He's an author, high impact teacher, and a Prophet of God.

Dr. White is a sought-after empowerment specialist, revolutionary thinker, and transformational leader. He has earned a distinguished reputation as a catalyst for change and voice of hope to nations.

Dr. Cedric White is a man after God's heart that loves His people. He is a leaders leader, an avid application preacher who is a known trailblazer by young preachers and Pastors predominately in Texas. In 1993, Dr. White was called to Texas to start a ministry in Texas with wife and Pastor Tangela White. The two were faithful and left

Louisiana for Texas, bringing their family, and birthing The Healing Place Church.

The church is a non-traditional church, equipped to address modern issues, and societal needs. The multi-cultural mission is accomplished in the physical setting and with ministries beyond the walls. Dr. Cedric White is the proud father of 6 Cedric Jr., Justin, La"Brandon, Tiffany, Tiana, and Aaron Jr.

Dr. White travels worldwide partnering with social, spiritual, and civic leaders in an effort to equip people everywhere to discover their purpose. He believes when people determine their purpose they can maximize their potential and leave a positive footprint. Viewing this world as a global village, he continues to initiate strategic interdisciplinary forums, as well as host conferences and summits. These events are designed to explain the simple solutions outline in the Word to work about solutions and healing to social and spiritual ills.

Upcoming Books by Dr. Cedric White include *The Giant Killers*, *As a Man Thinketh*, and *Living the God Nature*.

www.ingramcontent.com/pod-product-compliance
Lightning Source LLC
Chambersburg PA
CBHW072153020426
42334CB00018B/1984